RoosevElvis

the TEAM

ROOSEVELVIS

**CREATED BY RACHEL CHAVKIN, LIBBY KING, JAKE MARGOLIN AND KRISTEN SIEH
WITH MATT HUBBS, ANDREW SCHNEIDER AND NICK VAUGHAN**

OBERON BOOKS
LONDON

WWW.OBERONBOOKS.COM

First published in 2015 by Oberon Books Ltd
521 Caledonian Road, London N7 9RH
Tel: +44 (0) 20 7607 3637 / Fax: +44 (0) 20 7607 3629
e-mail: info@oberonbooks.com
www.oberonbooks.com

A catalogue record for this book is available from the British
Library.

PB ISBN: 978-1-78319-819-1
E ISBN: 978-1-78319-818-4

Front cover photo by Rachel Chavkin;
back cover photo by Kevin Hourigan

Printed, bound and converted
by CPI Group (UK) Ltd, Croydon, CR0 4YY.

RoosevElvis **was created in partnership with** The Bushwick Starr, London's Almeida Theatre and Gate Theatre.

It was made possible with support from The Jerome Foundation, The Drama League, A.R.T./New York Creative Space Grant supported by the Andrew W. Mellon Foundation, and with public funds from the National Endowment for the Arts, The New York State Council on the Arts with the support of Governor Andrew Cuomo and the New York State Legislature, and the New York City Department of Cultural Affairs in partnership with the City Council.

It was developed at The Bushwick Starr, the Almeida Theatre, and through The Drama League Artist Residency Program.

RoosevElvis **could not have been developed without the help and support of the following individuals:** Brenda Abbandandolo, Jon Adam Ross, Lauren Adleman, Akiko Aizawa, Danielle Amedeo, Victoria Andujar, Jean Andzulis, Joe Angio, Sarah Anton, Stephen Arnoczy, Peter Aspden, David Baloche, Nick Benacerraf, Shakti Bhagchandani, Paula Marie Black, Jeremy Blocker, Chris Bowser, Shannon Cameron, Lorne Campbell, David Cannon, Chris Cariker, Eileen Casterline, Herbert and Shirley Chavkin, David Chavkin, Cosmin Chivu, James Clark, Libby Clearfield, John Collins, Coney Island Lunch Room, Hannah Cook, Will Detlefsen, Bridgette Dunlap, Jason Eagan, Jerome Ellis, Dina Emerson, Andrew Farmer, Amanda Feldman, Brian Ferguson, Douglas Filomena and The Lightning Syndicate, Iona Tallia Firouzabadi, Desiree Fischer, William Fisher, Kay Fowles, Jeffrey Frace, Andrea Frankie, Francisco Frazo, Kate Freer, Anna Frenkel, Sarah Gancher, Vallejo Gantner, Joshua Gelb, Megan Ghiroli, Nancy Gibson, Gian-Murray Gianino, Kathryn Grody, Dan Hawkins, Chris Haydon, Jake Heinrichs, Leah Herman, Jeremy Hersh, Hildebandt's Restaurant, James Hill, Anna Hodgart, Jerry Homan, Stephanie Bok and ART/NY, Carly Hoogendyk, Lucy Jackson, Feygele Jacobs, Stephanie Janssen and Wally Krantz, Jake Jeppson, Stephanie Johnstone, Howard and Janet Kagan, Emily Kaplan, Meg Kelly, Bob Kelly, Jaime Karate King, Betsy King, Alex Koch, Nathan Koch, Tommy Kriegsmann, Barbara Lanciers, Robert

Landau, Susan Lang, Seán Linehan, Dave Malloy, Lauren Marks, Rebecca Martinez, Johannah Maynard, Barbara McAdams, David Mcgee, Annie McVey, Thya Merz, Lila Neugebauer, Laura Newman, Emily Perkins, Megan Riordan, Michael Rohd, Sara Rosenbaum, Ellen Rosenbaum, Edith Rosenbaum, Dan Rothenberg, Nina Rubin, Leanne Russo, Julian Sands, Magin Schantz, Richard Schechner, Noah Schechter, Lucia Scheckner, Jenny Schwartz, James Scruggs, Chris Shelley, Risa Shoup, Caitlin Sieh, Sarah Simmons, Kristin Slaysman, Austin Smith, Carol Tambor, Dave Tennent, Rusty Thelin, Jake Thomas, Nick Thomas, Stephanie Thompson, Paul Thureen, Traci Timmons, Annie Tippe, Chloe Treat, Ricardo Trindade, Emily Watson, Ric Watts, Stuart White, Lily Whitsitt, Peter Wiese, Jenny Worton, Nathan Wright, Jackie Wylie, Guy Yedwab, Pirronne Yousefzadeh, Mohammad Yousuf, and the rest of the members of the TEAM.

A particular thank you to the individuals and locations that hosted us during our filming road trip, including but not limited to Rose and David Ross, Larry Feerhusen and the staff of DelGould Meats, Lisa Feerhusen-Gunter, Jason Soukup and LaSon, Kay Fowles, Wall Drug, and the Motel Cortez.

The World Premiere of *RoosevElvis* took place at The Bushwick Starr, Brooklyn on October 7, 2013 with the following cast:

ANN/ELVIS PRESLEY, Libby King
THEODORE ROOSEVELT/BRENDA, Kristen Sieh

Rachel Chavkin, *Director*
Andrew Schneider, *Director of Photography/Editor, film sequences*
Jake Margolin, *Associate Director*
Nicholas Vaughan, *Scenic Design*
Kristen Sieh, *Costume Design*
Matt Hubbs, *Sound Design*
Austin Smith, Joe Cantalupo, *Lighting Design*
Joe Cantalupo, Andrew Schneider, *Video Design*
Kevin Hourigan, *Assistant Director/Production Stage Manager*
Dave Polato, *Development Stage Manager*
Genevieve Taricco, *Assistant Stage Manager*
Chimmy Anne Gunn, *Technical Director*
Jon Bremmer, Stephen Arnoczy, *Video Support*
Ethan Itzkow, *Lighting Operator*
Kailee Ayyar, Liz Rogers, *Run Crew*

Manda Martin, *Producing Director*
Lucy Jackson, *General Manager*
Anna Hodgart, *Producing Associate*
Meg Kelly, *Producing Assistant*
Madeline Bugeau-Heartt, *Producing Assistant*

the TEAM

The TEAM is a Brooklyn-based ensemble dedicated to making new work about the experience of living in America today. Once described as "Gertrude Stein meets MTV," the TEAM's work crashes American history and mythology into modern stories to illuminate the current moment. We combine aggressive athleticism with emotional performances and intellectual rigor, keeping the brain, eyes, and heart of the audience constantly stimulated.

Founded in 2004, The TEAM has created and toured 9 works nationally and internationally. We are four-time winners of the *Scotsman* Fringe First Award, Winner 2011 Edinburgh International Festival Fringe Prize, 2011 *Herald* Angel, 2008 Edinburgh Total Theatre Award, Best Production Dublin Fringe 2007, and were nominated for the 2012 Drama League Award for Outstanding Musical. The TEAM was recently cited on "Best of 2013" lists on 3 continents, and is a recipient of the American Theatre Wing's 2014 National Theatre Company Grant.

The TEAM has performed all over New York (including the Public Theater, PS122, and the Ohio Theatre); nationally (including the Walker Art Center in Minneapolis, and the A.R.T. in Cambridge); and internationally (including London's National Theatre, Barbican Centre, Almeida Theatre, and Battersea Arts Centre; Edinburgh's Traverse Theatre; Lisbon's Culturgest; the Salzburg Festival; the Perth International Arts Festival; and the Hong Kong Arts Festival).

The TEAM is Jessica Almasy, Frank Boyd, Rachel Chavkin, Stephanie Douglass, Jill Frutkin, Brian Hastert, Jake Heinrichs, Matt Hubbs, Libby King, Jake Margolin, Dave Polato, Kristen Sieh, and Nick Vaughan.

Artistic Director: Rachel Chavkin
Producing Director: Manda Martin
General Manager: Lucy Jackson

138 South Oxford Street
Studio 1C
Brooklyn, NY 11217
theteamplays.org

vimeo.com/theteamplays
facebook.com/theteamplays
twitter.com/theteamplays
instagram.com/theteamplays

Cast of Characters

ANN
a meat-processing plant worker in Rapid City, South Dakota

BRENDA
a taxidermist from Medora, North Dakota

ELVIS PRESLEY
singer/musician, rock 'n' roll icon
(played by the performer who plays ANN)

THEODORE ROOSEVELT
26th President of the United States
(played by the performer who plays BRENDA)

A NOTE FROM ONE OF THE WRITERS

From my late teens through my early thirties I worked as a waiter in coffee shops, breakfast joints, restaurants and bars. I was pretty good at my job, I think in part because I constantly, half-consciously pictured myself in a movie – a movie in which, by learning the rhythm of keeping the coffee pots filled during a morning rush; by keeping simultaneous conversations going with several different tables, the kitchen staff, and the incessantly ringing to-go telephone customers; by timing cigarette breaks so that nobody noticed I'd left; in short, by mastering all of the small moves that make up the dance of a simple service job, I was part of a romantic, heroic progression. In this ongoing daydream of my life as a film, I generally pictured myself as a compilation of various film waitresses and some of the truly great waitresses I've worked with over the years – salty, brash, gorgeous, tough as nails, and a little bit tragic. My movie life was accompanied by a soundtrack ranging from the Judds, to Morricone, to the hauntingly lonesome theme song from Percy Adlon's *Bagdad Café*, Bob Telson and Javetta Steele's "Calling You."

ROOSEVELVIS, like all TEAM shows, was collaboratively written. At the beginning of development we knew only two things for certain: Kristen was going to play Teddy Roosevelt and Libby was going play Elvis Presley. We talked a lot about how we see ourselves in constant relation to icons of "greatness," regardless of our own potential, and about how we find both solace and inspiration in these imagined connections. We talked about how there are those who live their lives accompanied by an internal soundtrack and those who don't.

Film became a central component of the piece. Much of the action of *ROOSEVELVIS* takes place on film, shot largely on location during a road trip from the Badlands of South Dakota to Graceland in Memphis, Tennessee. The original production was set on a film soundstage replete with c-stand lights maneuvered by stagehands and an oversized green-screen. Ann's humdrum house was a series of naturalistic movie sets out of which Ann, Brenda, Teddy, and Elvis exploded on their road trips.

In the last couple of years I've stopped waiting tables and, perhaps coincidentally, I've stopped picturing myself in a movie of my life. In my imagination I look more or less like myself and not so much like a weathered diner waitress lit by soft, magic hour light. I've noticed that unless the radio is playing I don't imagine a running soundtrack underscoring my daily activities. I genuinely wonder whether Teddy Roosevelt and Elvis Presley pictured themselves through the eye of a camera and whether they heard a score for their internal biopics. I suspect they did, and as we approach the winter 2015 remount of *ROOSEVELVIS* with its glorious films and brilliant performances, I wish that I could somehow see the movies of these great men's lives as they imagined them.

– Jake Margolin, Fall 2014

A NOTE ON INSPIRATIONAL MATERIALS

RoosevElvis drew on a lot of different research (books, articles, films, YouTube videos), but three sources played particularly strong roles in shaping the play. Kristen was swept up by the first book of Edmund Morris's magnificent three-part biography of Teddy Roosevelt (*The Rise of Theodore Roosevelt/Theodore Rex/Colonel Roosevelt*) in 2008 when we were making *Architecting*. Her passion for Teddy became the seed for this show, and Morris' trilogy (which reads like a screenplay of the polymath president's exploits) became a major source for all of us. Libby brought Peter Guralnik's seminal two-part biography of Elvis Presley (*Last Train to Memphis/Careless Love*) into the room. She read to us about Elvis' intense bond with his mother, his complicated marriage to Priscilla (only 14-years-old when they met), and his yearning to be a great film actor like James Dean. We became fascinated by the threat that he posed to accepted societal binaries of race and gender. And then there's *Thelma & Louise*. During an early writing session Jake proposed that Elvis and Teddy go on a wild road trip in a convertible Cadillac, so naturally we began talking about Ridley Scott's masterpiece. To us, it's the quintessential buddy movie for our generation, and it was the first movie of its kind to feature two leading women; its aesthetics inform much of the play.

A NOTE ON THE PERFORMANCES

Kristen and Libby's embodiments of Teddy and Elvis were stylistically quite different from one another, and there was a constant slipperiness in performance, with nearly imperceptible shifts often marking transitions between characters. Throughout the video sequences in particular this slipperiness extended to the performers, leaving it ambiguous as to whether we were watching the actress, the character in South Dakota, or the icon.

From Kristen: Teddy has been one of my heroes for about a decade. I have great admiration for him and therefore approached playing him with warmth and empathy, rather than any kind of ironic remove. That said, he is definitely a clown. He throws himself into everything with absolute commitment. While I steeped myself in the facts of his life, the character I shaped has a quality of having been painted from memory rather than from life. The voice I created for him came mainly from written accounts of how he sounded (shrill, loud, grandmotherly, effete) rather than from recordings that are available. I thought Katherine Hepburn, with her aristocratic Connecticut upbringing, her big, Teddy-like teeth, and her way of making a meal of her words, would serve as an admirable voice-double for Roosevelt.

From Libby: It wasn't until I spent 4 weeks in Las Vegas in 2010 while we were developing *Mission Drift* that Elvis Presley became someone I thought long and hard about. I encountered him there on a daily basis and became specifically curious about Elvis Impersonators. I wanted to understand what brought them to Elvis and why they needed him, carefully approaching it without judgment. That's why Ann exists. Looking through Ann's eyes was my way into this world. Ann needs Elvis, believes in him, and connects with both his heroism and deep sadness. They meet on a very human level. This is how my "Elvis" was born. I also want to note the obvious component of androgyny in the play. It isn't only about androgyny in the physical sense, but also of the heart. I thought a lot about my own maleness and femininity and then just let it go blurry. This is a hero's journey. Both Elvis and Ann became my heroes. Enjoy.

"Do I contradict myself? Very well, then I contradict myself,
I am large, I contain multitudes."

Walt Whitman

The set is a combination of ANN's apartment in Rapid City, and a film set.

As the audience enters, the two actresses are lounging on the couch watching THELMA & LOUISE on ANN's television.

At top of show, they migrate to center stage, already in full drag. They sit and address the audience. Both competitive and warm.

TEDDY: I was born in 1858.

ELVIS: I died in 1977.

TEDDY: My father's name was also Theodore.

ELVIS: My mama's name was Gladys.
I liked to call her Little Baby.

TEDDY: I called my little sister Corrine "Pussy."

ELVIS: *(Laughs.)* Oh man. That reminds me out in Beverly Hills, we had a pool, we had a cabana and I installed a two-way mirror so I could watch the girls change into their bikinis.

Beat.

TEDDY: I had two sisters and a brother.

ELVIS: I was an only child.

TEDDY: My mother was from Georgia.

ELVIS: Actually I was supposed to have a twin brother, but he died at birth.

TEDDY: My first wife, Alice, died in childbirth.
I remarried 2 years later.
I was born in New York, New York.

ELVIS: I moved to Memphis when I was 14.

TEDDY: I went to Harvard when I was 17.

ELVIS: I graduated high school. I got a job driving a truck.
I was training to become an electrician.

TEDDY: I ran for New York State Assembly and I got it. I was only 23.

ELVIS: I was 19 the first time they played me on the radio. Man, nobody knew *what* the hell I was, you know? Folks were calling in going, "Who's that? Who's that?" So Dewey Phillips gets me to come down to the station for an interview, and the very first question he asked me was what high school did I go to.

Cuz, he wanted folks listening to know I was a white guy. I mean, I was unlike anything anyone had ever seen before. I really shook things up, man. *(Beat.)* I never wrote any songs that I sung.

TEDDY: I wrote 45 books! Not including journals published posthumously. I wrote in my journal nearly every day, editing as I went. I was also a voracious reader. I read tens of thousands of books, sometimes three in a day. I can have a conversation with anyone about anything. I am a part of everything I ever read.

ELVIS: If I hadn't been an entertainer I would have liked to been sheriff.

TEDDY: If I hadn't been the President of the United States, I would have gone into natural sciences. I love animals. I love to dissect things and categorize them. When I was President the White House was full of pets.

ELVIS: I had a chimpanzee named Scatter. He knew how to drive!

TEDDY: I had a horse named Manitou.

ELVIS: I had a horse named Bear.
I love Christmas and lasagna and meat.

TEDDY: I love my family, the fourth of July, meat, and guns.

ELVIS: I like to carry a gun.

TEDDY: Me too. Very much. I have many guns.

ELVIS: I liked to carry a gun right here. *(Points to sternum.)*

TEDDY: I shot thousands of animals. My first present to Alice was a lynx pelt rug.

ELVIS: I can't remember the first gift I gave Pricilla but I'm sure it had diamonds in it. I bought thousands of Cadillacs, and I'm real into karate.

TEDDY: I believe in exercise. Good masculine pursuits. Build up the body and the mind will follow, that sort of thing. My father taught me that. And you know, Henry Adams once said of me that I was pure act! He was terrified of me. *(Beat.)* My father was the best man I ever knew.

A quiet moment.

ELVIS: I really like you man.

TEDDY: *(Looks at him.)* Well that's a lovely thing to hear.

ELVIS: I mean it.

Silence.

TEDDY: *(Turning chair to him.)* Let's be honest one to the other. You don't really know me.

ELVIS: Sure I do.

TEDDY: *(As if talking to a child.)* We've spent the last three days together. You only know what I have presented to you in those three days. If you like me, you are either the type of person who generally likes people, or you are far too trusting of first impressions.

ELVIS: I liked you before. I read about you.

TEDDY leans back in chair giving him a dubious look.

Why'd you gotta say that, Teddy? Why can't you just take a compliment?

Pause as TEDDY decides whether to be genuine. He decides to be.

TEDDY: Because I think you're worthwhile Elvees.

ELVIS: *(Mimicking his voice.)* Well I guess you only know what you know about me in the last three days or however you said it or however you just put it, which kind of hurt my feelings.

TEDDY: *(Laughing at him.)* You're a pretty easy read Elvees.

ELVIS gives the audience a sly look, like "That's what he thinks."

ELVIS: You know, I had a thing you said up on the wall of my office. Before I even knew you, like I know you now.

TEDDY: Curious. I would not have expected that.

ELVIS: I liked to read it every day before I sat at my desk. Sometimes I'd read it out loud even though nobody was there. I kinda felt like I was talking to you when I was doing that. Like I would look in the mirror, and I'd talk to you. Like my own version of you. 'Cause in my version, you were taller.

TEDDY stands and assumes a more noble position.

You were bigger boned. "It is not the critic who counts." *(TEDDY makes a sound of recognition and approval.)* "Not the man who points out how the strong man tumbled, or where the doer of deeds could have done them better. The credit belongs to the man who is – "

TEDDY starts to speak along.

ELVIS and TEDDY: "Actually in the arena." *(TEDDY extends the final "ah" sound and the word turns into the sound of cheering crowds.)*

ELVIS: Go on Teddy.

Quiet music underneath – the first gesture of subtle cinematic scoring.

TEDDY: "Whose face is marred by dust, sweat and blood; who strives valiantly; who errs and comes up short again and again; who knows the great enthusiasms, the great devotions and spends himself in a worthy cause; who at the best knows in the end the triumph of high achievement, and who at the worst, if he fails, at least fails while daring greatly, so that his place shall never be among those cold and timid souls who know neither victory nor defeat."

(Beat.) What a great quote.

ELVIS: It's perfect.

Crashing sound of buffalo stampede. Both men stand like prairie dogs, realizing that they are about to be caught. Both strike chairs quickly and restore the living room, including turning off the television. They run upstage and exit.

Video Village (a cluster of large monitors modeled on a film studio editing suite) plays ANN AT WORK on one monitor and STATIC SHOTS OF MEAT PLANT on other monitor. A small monitor plays WAITRESS FOOTAGE, which is a very static/simple shot of a kitchen in the back of a diner, that runs the length of the entire show, and features the two waitresses we will meet later in the play during a quiet day at work.

Onstage ANN enters with grocery bag. Pulls out beer. Puts beer in fridge and takes one. Opens it. Takes a swig. AHHHH…Takes another swig. AHHHH… (This should sound just a bit like a crowd of screaming girls at a concert.)

ANN: You there?

A long pause. It should be unclear whether someone will answer, until ANN supplies the response.

ELVIS: Yeah. I'm here Annie. How was your day?

ANN: *(Takes a drink.)* Great.

ELVIS: Come on, Annie! You don't gotta lie to me.

ANN: Sure I do. You should really come to my work sometime. You wouldn't believe.

ELVIS: Well, I'd like that. You should invite me.

ANN: What have you been doing all day?

ELVIS: I've just been hanging around your house. Combing my hair. I read some of your magazines. You got all my favorites. I ordered some Mexican food. I got a chimichanga, beef. I ordered a flauta. Some pinto beans and some pee-ko de-gay-yo... You ready for tonight?

ANN: I don't know.

ELVIS: C'mon Annie! You gotta keep your chin up. The internet is going to open up a whole new frontier for you. You just gotta be ready. You never know who's gonna walk through the door – and when the right one asks you "What kind of music you play boy?" You answer "I play *everything.*"

ANN: What should I wear?

ELVIS: Well that depends on what kind of lady you got coming over.

Suddenly the sound of a shower. BRENDA speaks from shower offstage.

BRENDA: Did you say something?

ANN: *(Looks back at bathroom. A beat for the world to settle.)* Is the water hot enough?

BRENDA: Huh?

ANN: Did you figure out the hot and cold?

BRENDA: Yeah.

ANN: It's tricky.

BRENDA: I think I got it.

ANN: Well I'm doing dishes so let me know –

BRENDA: Huh?

ANN: Well I'm doing dishes so let me know if it gets too hot for you. Feel free to use my exfoliator.

BRENDA: Are you talking to me?

ANN: I said feel free to use any of the stuff in there!

BRENDA: OK.

ANN: I'm just gonna leave a clean towel out here for you.

BRENDA: Out there?

Shower turns off.

ANN: Uh. I mean I can give it to you if you –

A female hand reaches out from the door. ANN hands her an Elvis towel, folded.

BRENDA: Thank you.

BRENDA closes the bathroom door, and again shouts from inside. ANN washes dishes.

ANN: How often do you come down here?

BRENDA: To Rapid City? About three or four times a year just for these taxidermy conferences.

ANN: What's the craziest thing you've ever taxidermied?

BRENDA: One time a guy wanted two sheep fucking.

ANN: Gross.

BRENDA: Mostly I hate it when people wanna combine different species. Like that shit I basically refuse to do at this point. I can't even tell you how many Capricorn requests I get... like can you take this little lamb and sew this fish onto it? Or can you make me a pig shark? But mostly it's standard stuff.

ANN: Like prairie dogs?

BRENDA: Sure.

ANN: And rabbits.

BRENDA emerges.

BRENDA: Yeah although actually rabbits are some of the hardest animals to mount because they're so thin-skinned.

She moves quite close to ANN.

It's easy to just totally fuck up a rabbit. You're taller than I would have thought.

ANN: What do I have a short profile or something?

BRENDA: Nah. Your picture just made you seem more petite.

ANN: You're pretty much exactly what I thought from your profile. You smell good.

BRENDA: You got that from my profile?

ANN: No. I'm learning that now.

BRENDA: Because I smell like your shampoo and your body wash. And your exfoliator. So I think you might just be a narcissist.

ANN: No. I'm really not.

BRENDA: I would be.

ANN: What.

BRENDA: If I looked like you. I'd be a narcissist.

ANN: Come on.

BRENDA: I'm just gonna…

BRENDA reaches around ANN and turns water off.

ANN: I meant earlier. You smelled good earlier, before you smelled like my stuff.

BRENDA: I know what you meant. I was just messing with you –

ANN suddenly kisses BRENDA. They share a long kiss. ANN then goes back to washing dishes.

ANN: So you're down for a few days?

BRENDA: Yeah.

ANN: Do you have plans for the weekend?

BRENDA: Well I used some miles to change my flight so I could stay a little longer. Because I figured if this went well –

ANN: That's great. 'Cause I'm around.

BRENDA: *(Pleased.)* Can I borrow your toothbrush?

ANN: Sure.

BRENDA goes off again. Faucet sound from the bathroom.

BRENDA: Hey! Do you camp?

ANN: What? Like hiking?

BRENDA: Sure, like outdoors, stars –

ANN: I didn't grow up doing that kind of thing or anything.

BRENDA: If this date had gone crappy I was gonna spend the weekend camping in the Badlands.

ANN: Last time I was in the Badlands I was with some guys from work and we did like a 2am paintball war…it was pretty sweet.

ANN looks at a picture on the wall of Mount Rushmore. Holds a ukulele and strums absent-mindedly.

You ever been to Mount Rushmore?

BRENDA: Nope.

Faucet sound.

ANN: Sometimes I like to get really stoned and go to Mount Rushmore.

BRENDA: I'm not really into pot. It makes me sleepy.

ANN: It's pretty weird. Just these faces.

Faucet sound off.

BRENDA: *(Emerging from bathroom.)* I've just heard it's disappointing.

ANN: It's taller than you'd think.

BRENDA: *(Noticing ukulele.)* Do you play?

ANN: No, not really –

BRENDA: I'll go to Mount Rushmore. If you'll go camping in the Badlands with me after.

ANN: YES.

Horn honks. Fast transition.

FOOTAGE of ANN DRIVING RV alone. She circles in and picks up BRENDA.

Onstage:

ANN: Surprise!

BRENDA: Sure is!

ANN: Are you the kinda girl who likes surprises or doesn't like surprises?

BRENDA: Um, yes and no. Where did – is this yours?

ANN: Rented it! You ever ridden in one of these before?

BRENDA: Once. Have you driven one of these before?

ANN: Nah. Come on, look inside. My friend Dale and his wife have one of these. They've been all over the country in it, and they swear it's the best way to travel.

BRENDA: Isn't Dale the one you don't like?

ANN: Dale? No, he's all right. What do you think?!

BRENDA: It's luxurious, I guess.

ANN: I figured we'd hit Walmart and grab some stuff. It's gonna be so fun cooking in here. Real adventure. You probably do stuff like this all the time?

BRENDA: Not exactly like this but adventure sure.

ANN: *(Beat.)* You don't like it.

BRENDA: It's fine. It'll be weird. Let's go.

They flop onto couch, which ANN has pulled out clumsily into the space, and which will be treated as the RV in this road trip section. Sound of ignition. And they're off.

BRENDA: How long have you worked at your plant?

ANN: Uh...long time. Like 15 years?

BRENDA: Geez –

ANN: Yeah –

BRENDA: That must give you a unique worldview. Grinding animals into anonymity every day.

ANN: I guess it does make me think that we're all just made up of the same parts.

BRENDA: That's a long – They should give you a gold watch.

ANN: A lot of the guys that work there have –

BRENDA: What, did you start/ when you were a kid?

ANN: *(Overlapping.)* Pretty much right out of school. I got a job in the office as a receptionist and then they moved me to the floor –

BRENDA: That's a career shift.

ANN: Yeah. I always pictured being, like, a really great office manager. Or like, head of human resources.

Silence.

But you make more money on the floor...so.

Silence.

They said I'd be more "comfortable" there.

BRENDA: That's so messed up!

ANN: It's really okay. I get along with all the guys.

BRENDA: Did you say anything?

ANN: It was a long time ago...so...

BRENDA: Why didn't you stand up for yourself?

ANN: It wasn't really like that.

BRENDA: *(Beat.)* Hunh...

> *Sound of car stopping.*

> *ANN and BRENDA stand.*

> *VIDEO: Image of MOUNT RUSHMORE or TITLE CARD.*

ANN: It's been a really long time since I've been here not stoned. Their noses are all so different.

BRENDA: I have real questions about whether Jefferson's nose really looked like that because I feel like from paintings, it did not look like that. It's a very feminine carving of him.

ANN: Washington looks like Washington. Lincoln looks like Lincoln. Roosevelt kind of looks like Magnum P.I.

BRENDA: Yes he does!

ANN: His mustache is very Freddie Mercury.

BRENDA: *(Sung.)*
They are the champions my friends

BRENDA and ANN: *(Singing loudly together.)*
And they'll keep on fighting, 'til the end

> *BRENDA abandons ANN mid song.*

BRENDA: *(Overlapping with the still singing ANN.)* I feel like Teddy is the only one of those guys who'd be really psyched to see his face carved into a mountain. Like he would have just loved how it dominates the landscape. That was always his M.O.

ANN: How do you know that?

BRENDA: I'm from Medora, North Dakota where he had a ranch, so he's sort of a local celebrity. *(Beat.)* I don't like it. I don't like this. I feel weird actually about how gross I feel about this whole area right now.

ANN: It's great. Look at all the people here. It's great.

BRENDA: Yeah but it's not. The guy who drove me up from the airport was telling me that this whole area is still contested Lakota territory. So it just doesn't seem like a happy, family, place to me spiritually.

ANN: I guess I never really thought about it like that. I guess I just always thought about the one guy who did this. And he just wanted to do it so bad.

BRENDA: It just seems so unthinking and aggressive.

ANN: That's what I like about it.

Back on the road. Driving towards the Badlands.

Idyllic music.

VIDEO: Footage of ANN and BRENDA at the Badlands at sunset. Beautiful silhouettes against the big sky.

BRENDA: *(Quietly spoken onstage over the sunset footage and music.)* Where are we gonna park this thing?

ANN: I got us a reservation at an RV park... Okay. I spy with my little eye something that begins with "B."

BRENDA: Billboard for Wall Drug.

ANN: Wow. You're really good.

BRENDA: You just picked like the biggest flashiest thing out there.

ANN: Yeah.

Music rises from the RV radio.

Onstage ANN and BRENDA curl up on couch for a blissful night in the Badlands.

The next morning. Still on the couch, ANN and BRENDA watch the following short film as if they were in a movie theater.

VIDEO sequence: A GOOD DAY AT WALL DRUG.

On screen ANN and BRENDA wander thru the road-side colossus that is Wall Drug, South Dakota.

The sequence ends with VIDEO of BRENDA on the phone with her ex-husband. The conversation is slightly tense, and becomes more awkward when ANN enters the frame and watches from a distance.

Onstage the women set for diner scene.

The next scene is performed live, with footage of the AWKWARD SILENT DINER MEAL on VIDEO.

BRENDA: Can I talk to you about something?

ANN: Am I in trouble?

BRENDA: Why did you pull away when I tried to kiss you just now?

ANN: I don't think so.

BRENDA: Just now waiting for a table.

ANN: People were looking at us.

BRENDA: So what?

Silence.

You think you're the first gay person they've ever seen?

ANN: Can you keep it down.

BRENDA: *(Points at ANN.)* GAY PERSON.

ANN: Okay. Okay. Jeez man. Where's our food? I'm hungry.

BRENDA: I'm still surprised you'll order a burger at a place like this.

ANN: Why?

BRENDA: Because you know how gross it is.

ANN: I *like* meat.

BRENDA: Yeah but, like, diner meat?

27

ANN: I pretty much like all meat.

Silence.

So what's your husband do?

BRENDA: My ex-husband?

ANN: Yeah.

BRENDA: He's an Assistant Principal at a middle school.

ANN: I hated middle school.

BRENDA: Who didn't?

ANN: There were definitely people I knew who liked it.

BRENDA: Yeah, and none of them are doing anything interesting now.

ANN: How long were you married?

BRENDA: Oh god…4 years-ish? We met the summer I was living in Alaska. So, yeah, 4.

ANN: You lived in Alaska?

BRENDA: Yeah. You can make a killing out there in the summertime. I sold shellfish and beer. People come up whale boating and stuff. National Geographic tours. It's actually kind of horrible because this incredible environment is totally dependent on that economy, but also it'll ruin it, you know?

I used to work with a couple of ex-army rangers, Dan and…somebody. They led month-long hikes into the parks for actually competent people. I went on one one year. It's basically what I want to be doing with most of my time. I'd brought my gun to try to get a couple animals for myself but Dan had brought his rifle for protection. I thought that was really sexy. I'd never actually shot anything to protect myself. I've never actually been threatened by an animal and felt like I had to shoot it to protect myself. But I'd also never hiked in Alaska and you have to be careful about the grizzlies up there because they will chase you and they are really hard to kill. Have you read Lewis and Clark's journals? They run into Grizzlies basically constantly and kind of can't believe how many bullets it takes to kill them. There's this one bear they shoot at who escapes and they find him newly dead like 5 days later with 20 bullets in his lungs. They're just really angry boulders with fur, basically. And then they'd meet Native American braves wearing necklaces with the claws of the bears they've killed? And they're like, "This guy's basically killed a tank with a bow and arrow!" Incredible.

Anyway. We ended up startling a bear while it was eating, and it charged. And Dan stood completely still and raised his gun up and shot it right between the eyes. Like blood splattered on our clothes, it was that close.

I actually peed myself. And I was not the only one but I was definitely the only one who admitted it. Fuckin' bros. That was really terrifying. I thought I was gonna die.

ANN: You have something –

ANN gestures that BRENDA has something on her face.

BRENDA: Really? *(She wipes her face, pissed.)*

ANN: That sounds amazing.

BRENDA: It was.

ANN: I'd love to go to Alaska.

BRENDA: You should.

ANN: Yeah.

BRENDA: Really. You should just go.

ANN: Yeah. Totally.

They eat in silence.

BRENDA: How's the burger?

ANN: Fine. It's great.

BRENDA: *(Rising to go to the bathroom.)* When we get back to the meth lab – I mean the RV park. I want to try an experiment on you. I think I can convince you something about good meat if you let me try.

ANN: I'm pretty hard to convince about stuff.

BRENDA: I really thought from your profile that we would be...

ANN: What.

BRENDA: Nevermind.

ANN: What.

BRENDA: I guess it was the "Reach for greatness, accept nothing less" bit.

ANN: Oh... That's just something me and Dale say. It's about karaoke cuz we both suck at it. It's an inside joke. I don't know why I put that there. I thought it would be funny.

BRENDA: You. Are remarkably unbrave.

ANN: You've known me for 3 days.

Short VIDEO of CAMPFIRE plays. An awkward night of ANN and BRENDA sitting in silence around a campfire. ANN looks at BRENDA, and suddenly for a moment BRENDA looks a startling lot like THEODORE ROOSEVELT (including facial hair). ANN blinks, and sees BRENDA again, who is just staring at the fire.

Onstage ANN and BRENDA shift back to the RV.

Next morning as they drive back to Rapid City.

Deeply awkward and distant.

ANN: What airline are you flying?

BRENDA: Spirit.

ANN: You must have a lot of miles.

BRENDA: Not anymore.

ANN: You know I've never been on a plane?

BRENDA: Okay...

ANN: I think all the time about going to Graceland.

BRENDA: So when are you going?

ANN: I don't know.

BRENDA: Okay...

ANN: You know Elvis was afraid of flying?

BRENDA: *(Beat.)* I'll see ya Ann.

> *BRENDA exits and the PERFORMER takes position at mic to do the voice of the SPIRIT AIRLINES RECORDINGS.*
>
> *MUSIC (something depressing).*
>
> *VIDEO: ANN CLEANING RV.*
>
> *Video Village plays ANN AT WORK.*
>
> *WAITRESS FOOTAGE resumes playing on kitchen TV.*
>
> *Onstage ANN re-enters home. An echo of first entrance: back into the routine of life.*
>
> *ANN gets a beer from the fridge and dials.*
>
> *Pushes a button on phone to turn on speaker phone. We hear the Spirit Recording begin mid sentence.*

SPIRIT RECORDING: ...calling Spirit Airlines. Thank you for continuing to hold. All of our representatives are currently assisting other callers. Please remain on the line. Your call is important to us. One of our representatives will be with you shortly.

> *After a while on hold, ANN opens a beer and does "AHHHHs."*

ANN: You there?

ELVIS: Yeah I'm here, Annie. How was your day?

ANN: It sucked. I almost got my hand cut off by the buzz saw.

SPIRIT RECORDING: Travel booked over the phone with this representative is subject to processing fees. To avoid these fees please book online at www.spirit.com.

ANN: What've you been doing all day?

ELVIS: I've been exercising, man. I'm trying to get into show shape. I did 45 minutes of karate, 45 minutes of meditation. I did sit-ups. I did push-ups. And I did not order Mexican food. I ordered a salad.

I got a surprise for you. I ordered you some stuff on Ebay. I used your credit card. I hope that's ok.

Doorbell. FedEx box arrives.

ANN opens the package: Blue suede shoes, jeans, and a man's shirt ANN picks up the shoes.

ANN: Blue Suede Shoes.

SPIRIT RECORDING: Did you know you can earn up to 15,000 bonus miles after your first qualifying purchase with your new Spirit World Mastercard. To apply visit www.spirit.com and become part of our Free Spirit Family. Thank you for continuing to hold. One of our representatives will be with you shortly.

ANN begins to dress in mirror as hold music plays.

ELVIS: Do you ever feel like your life is on hold Annie?

Grabs beer. ANN begins "Ahhh's" while watching an Elvis movie on TV.

This gesture grows in level of aggressiveness/desperation. Finally the third "Ahhh!" transforms into the recorded sound of a screaming crowd of teenage girls.

ANN's eyes go wide at the vision of the crowd.

There they are. Hello ladies! How you doin' tonight?! *(To a girl in front.)* You should dye your hair black. I don't like blondes. Just ask Ann Margaret.

PERFORMER playing BRENDA jumps up from chair where she has been doing SPIRIT RECORDINGS, rips off costume to reveal 1950s swimsuit. Blasting music. Vicious, vicious dance based on the Ann-Margaret/Elvis dance from Viva Las Vegas, *but terrifying and exhilarating.*

During this sequence, ANN transforms into full ELVIS drag with the DANCER's help and encouragement.

Once fully transformed, DANCER exits and ANN addresses the screaming fans. This should be hallucinatory, as ANN plummets into impersonation (mic distortion, light flashes, etc.).

ELVIS: Those of you who've never seen me before will realize tonight that I am totally insane and have been for a number of years. They just haven't caught me quite yet. I would like to take a little bit of your time to tell you how it is from my side of the story. When I first started in this business I was a little bitty guy. I had a little bitty guitar, little bitty side-burns, little shaky leg. And the word was out and they were going, "Watch out! Watch out! He's a squirrel!"

Tried to corner me. Tried to cut my hair.

And later I went to New York. They're going, "Get 'em! Get 'em! He's just out of the trees." And then they put me on the *Ed Sullivan Show.* And they're filming me from the waist up and Ed Sullivan's going, "Uh…uh…uh…this boy's a freak." And then they put me on the *Steve Allen Show* and they put me in a tuxedo, they were trying to tame me down and they had me singing to a dog, so I'm singing *(Sings.)* "You Ain't Nothing but a Hound Dog," and that dog's in heat and it's going, "Huh, huh, huh." And I'm going "Watch out!" And Steve Allen's going, "Son of a bitch!" And I don't know what he's saying about me at the time so I'm saying, "Thank you, sir. Thank you very much."

Turns upstage, bends over and clears throat loudly.

Sorry man I got a frog in my throat. That's the first meat I've had all day.

So anyway when I started out I was just out of high school.

Makes smacking sound into mic.

And I was doing that into a microphone and they're going, "Get him out of here! He's a freak."

When I first started out I was driving a truck and I was training to be an electrician, but I was wired the wrong way baby. Anyway, one day on my lunch break I went into a little recording studio to make a girl…make a record. Anyway I was doing that for my own purposes. I really wasn't trying to get into the business.

And about a year and a half later, that guy put that record out and everybody in town is going "Who's he? What is he? Is he? Is he?" And I'm going, "Am I? Am I?"

Panting. Looks around to try to find the source of the panting. Realizes it was him all along.

Dropping slowly back into ANN.

What is that? Oh it's me.

Spirit Phone Call goes through and rings. ANN races to pick up.

ANN: Hello? Ok we need to talk about your estimated wait time.
Uh…I would like to get a price quote on a flight.
Yeah. From Rapid City to Memphis.
No Rapid City. South Dakota.
Well, I'm surprised you don't have a direct flight two or three times a day…

The joke doesn't go well.

Oh for, um, tomorrow?
Tomorrow or the next day?
(Touch of ELVIS voice.) Well I guess I'm just an impulsive kinda person, you know?

Looking directly into mirror.

Well that's around what I thought it was gonna be…so… um…

I just have to check with my friends and I'll call back.

No, you have a nice day.

Hangs up phone.

Crosses to sit on couch. Buries face in hands.

ELVIS: Annie…come on, Annie.

ANN: Yeah.

ELVIS: I know you're trying. You've just been so good to me, sharing your world with me, letting me…you know eat your Cheez-Its and…you know, watch your TV, and all. I would like to return the favor. Not because I feel obliged… but because I really *want* to.

I've…I've been wanting to show you my house. I think you could use a few days of just lounging around there, watching all the TVs, eating all the food.

Graceland is a residence of the heart. It is far more than a place of physical needs Annie. To me it's all wound up with the acts of kindness and gentleness that my momma and my daddy lovingly provided. All that love remains in its walls. It's an enduring way of life for me. And I want you to see it.

Doorbell.

ANN sits up.

Knocking.

ANN stands.

Crosses slowly towards the door, stares at it, suspicious.

The door opens on its own.

TEDDY: Good evening. *(Enters with a lion pounce.)* I'm your hero's hero.

ANN has no idea how to respond.

Thank you for inviting me to dinner, it was ever so kind of you.

ANN: ...No trouble. Just making some pasta.

TEDDY: Oh, I adore the stuff! I love Italy, don't you? Pasta may be a humble dish, but it's hearty. It'll do you good. Da vero?

ANN: Sure.

TEDDY: *(Presents package.)* I took the liberty of bringing you this.

ANN: I feel like I should'a bought us a bottle of wine.

TEDDY: Not at all, not at all. I rarely touch the stuff.

ANN: Do you mind if I have a beer?

TEDDY: Oh I adore beer!

ANN gets two beers from fridge and hands one to TEDDY.

TEDDY: Ah, the laboring man's draft.

Beat. TEDDY and ANN both swig.

ANN does a small AHHHH, but TEDDY trumps ANN, turns to audience and crosses all the way downstage, with his arms up in triumphant pose, sustaining AHHHH as long as he can.

After a beat:

ANN: Please, have a seat.

TEDDY: If you'll join me.

ANN: Sure. *(They sit, measuring each other.)*

TEDDY: You look lovely this evening.

ANN: Thanks, Teddy.

TEDDY: Are you packed?

ANN: What?

TEDDY: Graceland. Memphis, Tennessee. We're going to Graceland. *(He leans in.)* Courage Ann. Elvees is waiting outside in the vehicle.

TEDDY stands and growls like a revving engine. This is matched with the sound of a car engine roaring into action.

Music! High Energy.

He runs to get the other rowing machine - the two rowing machines will be treated as ANN's car during this road trip section. ANN meanwhile opens the present TEDDY has brought, finds a man's gold watch, and puts it on.

ANN makes full transition to ELVIS, including wig.

TEDDY: *(Onstage while rowing exuberantly.)* Lean into it, Elvees.

ELVIS: Like this?

TEDDY: Oh, Elvees, you're so louche! You look like you've got nowhere to go in the world.

ELVIS: Well I don't, man.

TEDDY: Well pretend you do. Your languor is obscene. Here is your country!

On VIDEO screens backgrounds shift. And shift again as the road trip montage continues.

Have you been in the military?

ELVIS: Yeah man, in Germany.

TEDDY: But did you see action?

ELVIS: I drove a truck.

TEDDY: But you can fire a weapon?

ELVIS: Oh, yeah.

TEDDY: Can you fight with a knife?

ELVIS: Come on, man.

TEDDY: Mountaineering or wilderness survival? Anything out of doors?

ELVIS: Well we were dirt farmers.

TEDDY: *(Laughing.)* Dirt farmers?

ELVIS: Is that funny man?

TEDDY: Well you don't really have to grow it.

ELVIS: Rich kid.

TEDDY: No no. I understand your struggles. Ever engage in any scientific inquiry?

ELVIS: You're making me itchy, man. No!

TEDDY: Boxing? Show me your moves, Elvees.

TEDDY and ELVIS pull sharply off the road – sound of screeching tires. They launch into a jubilant series of trading physical demonstrations: TEDDY boxes and ELVIS does karate. Both use each other as foils, but speak directly to the audience. Showing off.

TEDDY: It was my second year at Harvard and while I had exercised my way from a thin-chested asthmatic child into a moderately well-built 19-year-old, I was not yet the barrel-chested cowboy that you know from the newspapers.

As a lightweight member of the collegiate boxing team I was engaged in a match of some import. My colleagues were all in attendance and my adversary was hard of hearing, perhaps from a lifetime of fisticuffs to the ear.

At one point, the bell had rung *(DING)* and he didn't hear it…

ELVIS, wherever he is in his karate demonstration, stands in front of TEDDY and punches him in the face.

Sound of booing and hissing fans.

The crowd went wild, I can tell you. They wanted him thrown out. But I said, "It's alright! It's alright! He didn't hear it! He didn't hear the bell!" Well they just thought that was the best thing they'd ever heard. They admired me ever since. What a great story I just told.

TEDDY goes to get old boxing gloves.

ELVIS: I began my karate practice when I was in the army in Germany. My momma didn't want me to do sports much, but she had passed away so – I left Germany with a black belt in karate. But it wasn't until I met Ed Parker out in Beverly Hills that I went deep. He was a Mormon. He was from Hawaii. He was an American karate master. But the part of his teaching that really took me there was the spiritual guidance that he added to the practice. You know, about readiness. Animal type readiness. And that's why I had the TIGER embroidered on all my gees, and of course my signature, the TCB with the lightning bolt, which stood for Taking Care of Business in a Flash.

As a button to this scene, ELVIS punches TEDDY in the face again. TEDDY squeals.

What a great story I just told man!

TEDDY: One time, on a sojourn through the Dakota Territories I came face to face with a great grizzly – about eight steps away. I raised the muzzle of my rifle toward him and shot him fairly between his two sinister eyes.

ELVIS: I had two career knockouts in my career. The first: a jealous husband out in Toledo. The second: a 6'4" gas station attendant and his friend. I approached the taller gentleman, he was smoking a cigarette.

ELVIS approaches an audience member, whispers in their ear, gives them a cigarette.

I displayed my karate prowess by doing a simple roundhouse kick, and knocking the cigarette clean out of his hand.

ELVIS " kicks" the cigarette out of audience member's hand.

(To audience member, if necessary.) Throw it man.

I was clearly acting in self-defense and I was not charged in either case.

TEDDY: *(Amidst some spectacular jump roping.)* One night in Mingusville, a drunken cowboy with a gun in each hand decided to ridicule me on account of my spectacles. I flattened him with one punch.

ELVIS: On August 26, 1970, an anonymous phone call came into the International Hotel Security Office – *(To STAGE MANAGER in booth.)* You're gonna need to turn this down, this is a very serious story. *(To deck crew.)* I'm gonna need some space, baby.

Music cuts out.

There was a plot to kidnap and assassinate me. The FBI was called in. I told my boys, "If anything happens to me I want you guys to get him. I want you to rip his goddamn eyes out. I don't want him sitting around afterwards like some Charlie Manson fella smilin' sayin', 'I killed Elvis Presley.'" I cried into my daddy's arms that night. Before I went onstage, I put a pistol in each boot. Midway through, a man from the balcony cries, "Elvis!" I flinched, man – I thought THIS IS IT – but he just wanted to request his favorite song. *(Beat.)* I felt obliged to bring karate to the world!

ELVIS launches into massive karate training dance sequence. Music blasts.

While ELVIS does dance, TEDDY slowly crosses onto couch and eventually cuts off choreography with lion roar and accompanying snarl sound effect. TEDDY crosses to and climbs on ELVIS' back, who has assumed a turtle-like protective position.

TEDDY: I refused to go about guarded. During a campaign speech I took a bullet in the right breast. I continued to orate for another hour with that bullet in me. And I did not perish. *(Roar.)* I will not abide anarchists!!

TEDDY scalps ELVIS (removing his wig) and stands triumphant in the silence, awkward. After a few beats.

Matty! Play my *Planet Earth* video!

VIDEO: sweeping images of the plains and bison. TEDDY, giddy at the sight, once again yanks on his boxing gloves and proceeds to box the projected images of the buffalo. At the climax of this absurd sequence, he throws off his gloves and launches into fierce ballet choreography. A stunning, seriously performed solo.

It ends with a bow, applause.

TEDDY joins ELVIS back in the "car." Quiet. It feels like they have been driving a long time in silence.

VIDEO: footage of the Badlands passing by.

ELVIS: Where are we man? *(Pause.)* It's pretty spooky. *(Pause.)* It looks like hell.

TEDDY: What hell would look like with the fires put out. "Les mauvaises terres a traverser."

ELVIS: I don't speak french.

TEDDY: "Bad lands to walk across," Elvees. The Badlands.

ELVIS: We're in the Badlands again?

TEDDY: The Badlands.

ELVIS: Annie said to wake her up when we're past here.

A quiet beat.

TEDDY: It looks the way Poe sounds, don't you think?
"Ah, broken is the golden bowl! The spirit flown forever!
Let the bell toll! – a saintly soul floats on the Stygian river;
Come, let the burial rites be read – the funeral songs be sung:
An anthem for the queenliest dead that ever died so young,
A dirge for her the doubly dead in that she died so young."

41

VIDEO: Flashes of ALICE ROOSEVELT in the Badlands (played by the same actress portraying TEDDY).

ELVIS: What are you thinking about, Teddy?

TEDDY: I don't want to talk about dead people.

ELVIS: *(Beat.)* It's crazy out here man. It's like…
Green.
And brown.
And green…

TEDDY: Well put.

ELVIS: Hey man. Pull over at this diner. I gotta go pee.

TEDDY: Wonderful, I'll go climb something.

Sound of screeching wheels.

VIDEO: Static Shot of a Waffle House. The stream of WAITRESS FOOTAGE which has been playing quietly since near the top of show jumps seamlessly to link up with the scene as played live – as if the two parallel universes of stage and video come together for this one moment.

Green screen opens to reveal TEDDY (DENEESE) and ELVIS (LYNNE) now wearing waitress dresses. They stand a long time in silence, as during a slow afternoon at the diner.

LYNNE: Well she just shouldn't…

DENEESE: What. Say it.

LYNNE: I'm just saying…

DENEESE: I know.

LYNNE: I mean: If you don't want to work, don't show up, you know?

DENEESE: I know.

Blackout.

VIDEO sequence: ANN in the car, looking into the rearview mirror. WAITRESS, played by the same actress who plays BRENDA, steps into sightline. (The video echoes the first establishing shot of Brad Pitt in THELMA & LOUISE.*) Whereas TEDDY and ELVIS may have looked ridiculous in their hastily-put-on waitress costumes, the WAITRESS in video should look both lovely and unremarkable. ANN watches her, and imagines their eyes meeting. Romantic.*

Onstage ELVIS enters and watches the VIDEO of ANN watching the WAITRESS. He sings "Love Me Tender" quietly. His singing blends in with the sound of the song, which is playing on the radio in ANN's car in the VIDEO.

ELVIS: *(Singing.)*
   ...And I always will.

The song continues live and recorded.

In the VIDEO, a long moment of ANN fantasizing a shared romantic gaze with the WAITRESS while the song plays. Then the WAITRESS walks by ANN's car without noticing ANN and exits the frame.

Onstage TEDDY re-enters.

ELVIS: *(To – unseen – waitress passing by.)* Hey.

TEDDY: What's going on?

ELVIS: I'm just flirting man.

TEDDY: I recognize that look.

ELVIS: I'm sure you do Teddy.

TEDDY: No. That is the look when you spot the perfect cerulean warbler. That look of "Oh, I want it. I want it. I want to kill it. I want to take it apart and put it back together again and put it in a glass jar."

ELVIS: No man, I just wanted to know her, you know? She's the kind of girl who could just...calm...me...down. The way the wind moved the skirt across her thigh. The way she closed her eyes against the bright sun. She could've of

43

been the love of my life. *(Beat.)* Hey man, what hotel we staying at tonight?

TEDDY: Hotel? *(Laughs.)*

A mood shift. We are going off road into nature.

VIDEO: Slow motion. ELVIS and TEDDY walking thru the woods. Beautiful. Quiet.

Transitions to VIDEO: TEDDY kayaks slowly across a river.

VIDEO: On Video Village one screen shows TEDDY expertly setting up a tent, and other shows ANN disastrously setting up a tent.

ONSTAGE: ELVIS exits.

Bird sounds. TEDDY sits on one of the rowing machines (which have become logs) and does birdcalls, trying to translate various birdcalls to English.

Time passes.

Nighttime. A campfire. ELVIS re-enters with ANN's ukulele and a hot dog for TEDDY.

The men sit backwards on the rowing machines.

ELVIS: You ever talk to people Teddy?

TEDDY: Of course I talk. I talk all the time.

ELVIS: No, I mean… *(Laughing.)* You do. You talk all the time. *(Shaking it off.)* But, I mean, like, in your head?

TEDDY: I still hear my father's voice sometimes.

ELVIS: I hear my Little Baby. *(TEDDY looks at him.)* My momma. But that's different… I mean, do you ever make up conversations in your head? Like how, how Annie talks to me.

TEDDY: No!

ELVIS/ANN goes upstage, embarrassed. Opens fridge and gets a beer. TEDDY thinks for a while. Then:

TEDDY: Hiya John.

ELVIS: *(Excited.)* Who's John?

TEDDY: John Muir.

ELVIS leaps toward TEDDY.

ELVIS: Who's John Muir?

TEDDY: John Muir's my hero. Hiya John. How's it going? How's the family?

JOHN: *(TEDDY becomes JOHN MUIR, complete with Scottish accent.)* I wouldn't know, they're in Scotland. Seems fine.

TEDDY: Oh that's too bad, that's too bad John.

JOHN: A life in the wild. You know, it's a consummation devoutly to be wished. You're just out there, and there's just you and your manhood and your humanity, with all that plant and animal life and your family is the wilderness I guess.

TEDDY: Look at those stars, John. I'm going to memorize them. What's that one?

TEDDY points to the sky.

JOHN: Cassiopeia.

TEDDY points.

TEDDY: What's that one?

JOHN: The Painter.

TEDDY points.

TEDDY: And that one?

JOHN: The Sculptor.

TEDDY points.

TEDDY: That's the Pleiades.

TEDDY points.

JOHN: Ay.

TEDDY: And that's – that's Orion. With his little belt and Beetlejuice on his shoulder.

JOHN: Ay. You know I'd like to take this opportunity to tell you I like what you're doing Teddy. I think you're a good guy. I think you're a really good guy. I like your clothes. I think you've got a good heart. Like, a good spirit, like you're a good hard-working kind of guy. We could use your kind of guy around here. Why don't you come out here? Why don't you come out to California, herd sheep with me. You can live in my wee cabin with me. It'll be great. We could eat flapjacks every morning and have cowboy's coffee. Oh why don't you be my best friend?

TEDDY: Oh gosh! Oh that sounds just swell John! You mean it? But I think I'd get restless.

JOHN: Oh, I don't think you would.

TEDDY: I think I would.

JOHN: Well, I don't think you would.

TEDDY: I think I would.

JOHN: Well, I don't think you would.

TEDDY: See here now. I said I think I'd get restless. I have to keep up my contacts in Albany.

JOHN: But you couldn't.

TEDDY: Why not? I can do more things at once than anyone I've ever met.

JOHN: 'Cuz you'd miss the point.

TEDDY is deeply insulted. Crosses arms, and sulks quietly.

After a long silence.

ELVIS: He really likes you man. I mean…you can feel that. *(Presses heart.)* I had a lot of friends. They came to Graceland almost every day. We played football together on Sundays. I was always the quarterback. My team always won. I bought them things. Horses. Cars. I paid for their weddings. I employed them. My friends worked for me... My momma was my best friend.

TEDDY: When did she die?

ELVIS: She died right before I went into the army. I was so lonesome over there in Germany. I was so brokenhearted. I'd never had a broken heart before. I'd walk around so forgetful. So confused. I'd call out to her and forget she wasn't in the kitchen. I'd clutch my heart every time her spirit moved past me. You know that feeling?

TEDDY does. He doesn't answer.

When someone close to you dies you can feel 'em sweep past you like a gust a wind man. It's just like a thought – you know – or a memory or something familiar. I don't know how to describe it.

TEDDY: There's nothing like family. It's the only thing.

ELVIS: People said I had an unhealthy relationship with her. They said I was a momma's boy. Said it was weird how we talked to each other, said we talked baby talk. Said she got too close to my girlfriends. Said that we lived in our own private world. Man, she worshipped me and I worshipped her. It was so sad the day she died, walking out of the hospital – getting in the pink Cadillac that I got her – that she loved. And driving back to Graceland. Tears streaming down my face. Not caring if I crashed. Not caring about life, man.

THEODORE: I don't understand women. But somehow all of them, one's mother, one's sisters, one's wife...all contain a particular kind of hope. A particular kind of feeling for me... My mother and wife died on the same day. Valentine's Day, 1884. I just buried that feeling with those two women. Wiener?

Offering ELVIS the hot dog he has been roasting over the fire.

47

ELVIS: No thank you, Teddy. You know, you comfort eat. You better watch that.

ELVIS takes out ukulele. Begins to play and sing, "That's Someone You Never Forget."

ELVIS: **The way she held your hand...**

TEDDY: That's beautiful.

ELVIS: I wrote this for my little baby.

TEDDY: Well it's beautiful.

ELVIS: *(Resuming singing.)* **When She** –

...I came up with the title...my friend Red wrote the song.

ELVIS resumes singing and TEDDY joins in, singing a very light harmony on an "Ooh."

They continue the full song, and as they do, TEDDY does a bit of gentle hula.

ANN: I'm gonna go to bed.

ELVIS: G'Night Teddy.

ANN/ELVIS lays on sofa.

TEDDY: Sweet dreams Elvees...

TEDDY settles down. Perhaps to journal or write a letter. He hears something.

Alice?

Quiet music.

TEDDY slowly puts hand to head, removes buns, hair spills down, and he fans it around head.

ALICE: *(TEDDY becomes ALICE.)* Hello Teddy.

TEDDY: *(Stunned.)* My own sweet pretty darling.

An image flickers onto the television screens of ALICE, walking ghostly in the distance by TEDDY's campfire.

ALICE: How are you?

TEDDY: I am living in dreamland.

ALICE: Oh?

TEDDY: I'm living the life of a true cowboy darling and having a marvelous time. The other day after a hunt, we were so dirty we looked like two clay men descending two clay horses.

ALICE: Are you bathing regularly?

TEDDY: *(Whispered with a grin.)* No.

ALICE: It must be lonely out there.

TEDDY: You can turn around without stepping on the feet of others. With my horse and my Winchester rifle, I feel like a figure from other days.

ALICE: But aren't you lonely.

TEDDY: *(Overwhelmed.)* Oh Alice. The light has gone out of my life.

He begins to cry but suddenly puts his hands to his eyes and pushes the tears back. He rises, stomps around in circle. Does aerobic arms.

I have to climb something.

TEDDY exits.

ANN wakes up.

ANN: Oh… wow…

Wipes drool off of chin.

ELVIS: What is it Annie? You have a bad dream?

ANN: No. Not really bad. Just really… um – real. You know how sometimes you have those –

ELVIS: Oh I know Annie. I know. Sometimes I can't tell if I'm awake or asleep 'cuz my dreams have gotten so real feeling.

VIDEO: Slow transition to ANN's dream sequence. Hazy glimpses of the images described.

ANN: Yeah. I dreamed I was walking into work – it was just like always – past reception, say good morning to Mary – through the main office, keep my head down – take a right and down the hall to the the locker room but instead of the normal locker room door it was like an airport security check line with all these security guards and security cameras and CCTV screens, and the guards are pointing at me and laughing. And I see myself on those screens... and I'm naked and everyone can see the dude underwear I wear that are like baggy where my junk should be. But it's like instead of it being humiliating it's like this totally joyful thing. And so I start laughing and the guards who are all these hairy bald guys suddenly turn into like these perfect prim 14-year-old girls and they're dressed in security guard suits, but like girls from the Sixties, you know? And they start grabbing at their hair and screaming after me and running... Oh! And then I remember – I busted out onto the floor and started boxing with all of the cow carcasses like they're punching bags, like – from *American Gladiator* or like a carwash, and then I remember – and somehow I'm standing in HR and like for some reason Dale is conducting this interview and I start yelling at him...

ELVIS: What you were yelling?

ANN: I don't remember, but it felt amazing.

ANN stands suddenly.

I'm hungry. I'm really hungry right now. I feel like I only eat 'cuz it's time to eat, not 'cuz I'm hungry. I'm really hungry right now.

ELVIS: That's good, Annie. That hunger is something to ride. You gotta let it fill you up.

Music begins. A ramping up in energy.

'Cause we're gettin' closer. And the closer you get to something, the more fearsome it becomes. It's like when

the lights come on at the beginning of a concert. And –
boom – you can ride that wave of everyone screaming, like
a waterbed. And then you don't have to be just who you
are – you can be everyone else too. It's like touching the
sun.

*ANN/ELVIS rows furiously at the rowing machine. ANN sings along
with Elvis' "King of the Jungle," which is blasting from the car stereo.
It should feel like ANN is courageously on the road alone, and soaring.
ANN sings and rows for a while.*

*There is a huge hiss, bang, and steam comes out of the engine. The
rowing machine wheel spins slowly to a stop. ANN sits quietly in the
broken down car, as if it will start on its own.*

ANN: You gotta be kidding me. If this costs a lot... I should've
just flown.

ELVIS: You're scared to Annie.

ANN: I know. What a loser

A beat. Then wordlessly ANN begins to walk off.

TEDDY suddenly enters and blocks ANN's way.

TEDDY: Where are you going, Ann?

ANN: We're going to that motel we just passed.

TEDDY: Motel? *(ANN brushes past him to exit. Shouting after ANN.)*
But that's backwards. You can't go back! Elvees, don't
encourage her!

ANN: *(From offstage.)* This one had a pool.

Transition into the MOTEL.

*VIDEO: Footage of ANN jumping into the pool, swimming and
contemplative. On monitors: footage of ELVIS and TEDDY arriving
at the motel.*

*ONSTAGE: ELVIS enters from the motel bathroom and stretches, now
in silk kimono. TEDDY sits grumpy on bed.*

ELVIS: Don't be so pouty Teddy. Get into it. Relax.

TEDDY: Don't tell me to relax. This motel is frankly the physical manifestation of my existential Hell.

ELVIS: You're just bored, man. I'm ordering us some pizza.

ONSTAGE: ELVIS reaches into drawer of TV table and grabs phone book. Blackout.

VIDEO: ANN watches TV and gets pizza.

MOTEL TELEVISION: Plays THELMA & LOUISE *in the Blackout.*

ONSTAGE: Lights rise. ELVIS is on ANN's iPhone.

TEDDY: What are you getting into?

ELVIS: I'm just looking at Annie's Facebook page.

TEDDY joins him. Laughter of them looking at Facebook.

TEDDY: Oh go to that one! "Dale's Wedding Pictures." I wanna see this Dale fellah.

A moment as they look at Facebook page.

TEDDY: Robust sort of fellah, isn't he?

ELVIS: I knew he'd be bald.

Pause as they continue to look at ANN's Facebook.

TEDDY: Look at Annie's sister.

ELVIS: Annie doesn't have a sister.

TEDDY: Right here, Elvees.

ELVIS: That's Annie.

TEDDY: *(Stunned.)* No. Look at all that hair. Well I – I must confess, I had no idea she was beautiful.

Blackout.

VIDEO: ANN puts down pizza and turns on the shower.

MOTEL TELEVISION: Plays THELMA & LOUISE *in the Blackout.*

ONSTAGE: Lights up. TEDDY watches ELVIS, who is completely passed out.

TEDDY: Elvees. Elvees. Elvees. Elvees. Elvees. Elvees. Elvees. Ann.

Blackout.

VIDEO: ANN gets out of shower and eats pizza while watching TV.

MOTEL TELEVISION: Plays THELMA & LOUISE.

ONSTAGE: Lights rise on TEDDY practising a karate sequence that ELVIS has taught him. ELVIS is coaching from the side.

ELVIS: Woah, not like fencing man. Look at your legs. You look like a cricket. Try it again.

TEDDY pouts. Does the sequence again.

Closer. Closer. Okay. All right.

TEDDY: But close doesn't win the day, does it??

TEDDY tries again.

ELVIS: Ok man, you're getting just a few steps ahead of yourself.

TEDDY: No I was doing what you said. I was doing the chewey zuki.

ELVIS: Choku zuki.

TEDDY: Chewey zuki.

ELVIS: Choku zuki.

TEDDY: Chewey zuki. Choku zuki. I'm doing what you said.

ELVIS: No, it's about patience and technique.

TEDDY: You worry about your own patience. I'll worry about mine.

ELVIS: Man, you're like a grasshopper. You do everything so fast.

They continue doing moves.

TEDDY: What an absurd sport.

ELVIS: Karate is more than a sport man. It's a way of life.

TEDDY: *(Mocking him.)* It's a way of life.

ELVIS: It's like you refuse to engage if *you* didn't discover it
    or it wasn't your idea or whatever… *(TEDDY keeps fucking
    around.)* You're impossible to play with!

*ELVIS gets angry and stalks away as TEDDY prances around and
does karate routine and laughs.*

ELVIS watches this for a bit. Then:

You know I can't imagine being your kid. *(TEDDY stops.)*
    I mean what a nightmare.

TEDDY: How dare you. HOW DARE YOU! As if Lisa Marie
    is a picture of mental health and enlightenment – You want
    to talk about parenting? HA.

ELVIS: Just forget it man. I'm gonna work on my breathing.

TEDDY: You want to talk about patience and meditation
    and "Wait for the other man to strike first" and all that
    philosophical hoo-haw? *(Imitating ELVIS' breathing.)* People
    who breathe and people who – Let's talk about the people
    who DO and the people who WAIT.

TEDDY faces full front, in an echo of the opening image, sitting center.

You ever heard of Woodrow Wilson?

*During the following, ELVIS exits into the bathroom and ANN
emerges, crossing through the set. This is not remarked upon.*

ELVIS: *(Shouting from bathroom.)* Can't hear you through my calm
    Teddy.

TEDDY: Well you would have liked him. He was good at
    burying his head in the sand too! I can still hear his
    childish mewling: "it's not our problem" and "let the
    Europeans figure it out on their own." Well I told him

that the POINT of carrying a big stick is that you USE
that stick when the world calls out to you in convulsions
of genocide. That if we continue with soft complacency
to stand helpless and naked before the world, we shall
excite nothing but contempt and derision when disaster
ultimately overwhelms us!

ELVIS: We know you were a great president. Your face is on a
Goddamn cliff.

*During the following, ANN exits into bathroom and changes back into
ELVIS and re-enters with beer. Again, not remarked upon.*

TEDDY: Elvees I breathed my last breath in 1919 with the
knowledge that we had entered, fought, and won the War
to End All Wars, that we were men of action and had
secured for all freedom from Tyranny and from the ravages
of senseless war.

ELVIS: *(Re-entering.)* You're lucky you didn't live to see the next
50 years.

ELVIS sits next to TEDDY and competes for audience as well.

This position should now fully echo the opening scene of the show.

TEDDY: "Professor" Wilson was dilly-dallying because he had
no moral compass.

ELVIS: Maybe you just didn't understand Wilson's sense of
right and wrong.

TEDDY: Oh, I did Elvis. Like you, all he cared about was *ease*
and giving the people *what they want.*

ELVIS: And what's wrong with that?! You just walk around
giving people YOU DON'T EVEN KNOW what YOU
think they need.

ELVIS turns chair towards TEDDY.

Look, I know it comes from a big-hearted place, Teddy,
but you gotta understand that you're a very privileged
man and you're a little hard to be around when you get all
preachy like this.

TEDDY: I'm well aware of my many blessings and I believe I have lived my life with the utmost rigor to prove myself worthy of my cultural and financial inheritance.

ELVIS: All I'm saying is you have all the options in the world and some folks don't.

TEDDY: Well isn't that the pot calling the kettle black?

ELVIS: No it ain't. Because I didn't come from it. And that never goes away. People without means – and I'm not just talking about money here – get desperate. And while they're waiting for people like you to help them figure out what the hell they're supposed to do? They get crazy in their heads and before you know it, Bang!! That crazy's gonna find a way out!

TEDDY: Whatever you came from Elvees, you are a leader now. People look up to us, and that is a great responsibility. I spent my life and a great deal of my personal wealth helping those less fortunate.

ELVIS: *(Turns chair to face full front.)* So did I dummy.

TEDDY: But the social damage you did to earn that money –

ELVIS: *(Mocking him.)* Social damage.

TEDDY: What you've done is dangerous.

ELVIS: I'm an entertainer. You're goddamned right it's dangerous.

ELVIS stands and pulls back his kimono to reveal his underwear, gyrating his hips slowly.

TEDDY: You're a degenerate.

ELVIS moons TEDDY.

ELVIS: *(Really raging.)* Oh kiss my ass you suffocating prude.

Both TEDDY and ELVIS are standing now.

TEDDY: You watch your mouth!

ELVIS: You watch your own! I'm letting it all come out! Raw, man! Raw!

TEDDY: You *are* a degenerate –

ELVIS: You're a rich kid man! And you're afraid. You're just like them – you shut down anything you don't understand.

TEDDY: *(Continuing.)* And you're a whore. You just needed friends. And your "friends" found that out, and built a profiteering business on your back. It doesn't even matter what you do on stage anymore. You could fall down dead and people would pay more to see that than they would to see you sing!!! The people who like me think I can do something good for the world. The people who like you think that you're a good-looking fellow with a nice voice and a pair of hips. And I think that's sad. I think that makes you a show pony, and I'm a war horse. And yes, I think that's a better thing to be. So I'm sorry if my superiority offends you.

ELVIS: *(Deeply stung.)* You're just jealous 'cuz nobody here even remembers who you are! They all mistake you for your cousin or forget everything except that they named the Teddy Bear after you!

TEDDY: You want to take this outside?

ELVIS: Sure, COWBOY.

TEDDY: You "cowboy" yourself.

ELVIS: Come on.

They take it outside. Sounds of wild animals.

VIDEO: MANIC MOTEL SCENE with ELVIS and TEDDY running and jumping all over, throwing the motel room into complete disarray.

ONSTAGE: ANN quietly appears, caught in the light of a snowy television.

ANN watches the door, listening to TEDDY and ELVIS fight.

Takes out phone and dials.

As the phone rings, BRENDA appears in the doorway (the actress who plays TEDDY should just adjust hair, but otherwise remain in full chops and drag).

BRENDA: Hello?

ANN: Brenda. Hi. It's Ann.

BRENDA: Yes I know. Hi Ann. It's late.

ANN: I know. I'm sorry. I just –

BRENDA: You sound fucked up.

ANN: I am – a little.

BRENDA: Where are you?

ANN: I'm in a motel. My car broke down. And… And I'm not really sure what I'm gonna do. I'm. I'm on a journey now. I'm going to Graceland. I'm on my way to Graceland and Elvis Presley and Teddy Roosevelt are with me and we're staying at the Motel Cortez somewhere in the middle of Missouri. And I'm farther away from home then I've ever been and there is cherry wallpaper all over the walls which reminds me of you because – you smelled like cherries that first night when you came over. And I keep having this dream where I'm this other version of myself like my true self you know, where I showed up at work in my underwear and I'm boxing with all these cow carcasses, and then I'm in HR, and Dale is there, and before he can even say anything I yell. And my voice is like the sound of six people's voices at once, and I'm like – and I say – "I am unlike anything you have ever seen before." And I wish I was that person when we met. It's like in the dream I am so many people at once and I'm able to *show* it. And I wish that you weren't walking around Medora feeling sorry for me…Brenda?

BRENDA: Yeah Ann.

ANN: So Elvis told me this thing it's from a book called *The Impersonal Life,* he read it when he was lost, when he was on a search, I don't remember the story exactly but he said this to me: "We only got this moment together so let's have it completely, no holding back no wasting time on trivialities. I have the word and I can give it to you. I'm not a man I'm not a woman I'm a soul a spirit a force I have no interest in anything of this world I want to live in another dimension entirely." And you know I can't quite grasp it – but I think another dimension would be really good for me...or...

Brenda?

BRENDA: Yes Ann.

ANN: Um...what do you think of when you think of me? Do you think there is something wrong with me? Do you wish you had never met me or do you think of me and kinda vomit in your mouth a little bit or do you feel sorry for me or was I mistake or do you tell the story of us/our weekend together to everyone at the bar and they're all in hysterics thinking it's the funniest saddest story that they ever heard and you tell it so well and it's so funny you think to yourself man maybe I should have been a stand-up comedian or what... What do you think of when you think of me? Like do you think I'm capable of being loved? And do you – do you believe that people can change...

BRENDA: I don't know Ann. I mean do you really want me to tell you? Are you even going to remember this conversation? I think you are depressed. You should probably see someone. It's like you have been living in a cabin in the woods not talking to anyone or engaging with what's going on in the world. You are 35. It seems you graduated from high school and you went to college and you graduated from college and you got a job, and then you stopped. You just got your meat job and you went to work and you came home from work and you went to work and you came home from work and you went to work and you came home from work and then 15 years had passed. That's a great dream you described but in real life, you're not even comfortable, you're certainly not proud of being gay.

ANN: That's not really –

BRENDA: That's, I mean, you are not engaging with that conversation really. Which could be a really extraordinary or fucking triumphant thing – America's changing Ann, it's like "out." You don't have to be so scared… And yes, I did tell my big gay RV adventure story to all my friends at the bar the other night and they laughed so hard they peed, and I laughed so hard I cried, but other than that I haven't really thought about you that much.

But I am glad for you that you are on this trip – and I'm glad that when I think about you tomorrow I can picture you at Graceland instead of sitting on your couch getting stoned and watching *Blue Hawaii*.

BRENDA hangs up and exits.

ANN stands, quiet. Thinking.

After a long beat, ANN grabs car keys, and exits.

VIDEO: ANN driving to Graceland with directions from Google maps. Quiet. No soundtrack other than the recorded voice giving directions.

ONSTAGE: Eventually ELVIS and TEDDY enter, holding each other by the shoulders, jovial.

ELVIS: You really nailed that Choku Zuki, man.

TEDDY: You're an animal Elvees!

ELVIS: I know. I'm a tiger.

They look around for ANN, and see VIDEO of ANN DRIVING on the MOTEL TELEVISION. They stand and watch. After a while:

TEDDY: Oh, good for her.

TEDDY starts to strike the couch, which had folded out to become the motel bed.

ELVIS: *(Still glued to the television, urging her on.)* Turn the music up Annie! Sing at the top of your lungs, girl! That's the way! Drive.

ELVIS watches VIDEO of ANN DRIVING for a while, which remains quiet. No soundtrack.

Eventually ELVIS joins TEDDY in cleaning up and striking the motel as they play the following scene:

TEDDY: Small triumphs. You know, I could always see what kind of man I would be. I was born hungry. When I was eight my nanny said I'd be president.

ELVIS: I always saw my life like it was a movie. Ever since I was a little kid.

TEDDY: I always saw myself riding a horse. I mean whenever I picture myself, I picture myself on a horse.

ELVIS: I always pictured myself in a convertible with the top down.

TEDDY: And *tall.* I always pictured myself tall.

ELVIS: I always pictured myself with a gun.

TEDDY: Oh, yes indeed I always had a gun.

They look approvingly at one another.

Where did you picture yourself? On a concert stage? – oh, this is *fun,* Elvees!

TEDDY sits in director's chair by Video Village.

ELVIS: I always picture myself in my jungle room. Sitting with my little baby, and also with Priscilla.

TEDDY: I always pictured myself standing on the edge of the Grand Canyon... On the edge of something so vast that it could not have been made by the hand of man. I always picture myself in the presence of the work of God.

ELVIS: I love the Grand Canyon. It's really big. I always feel so big, you know, standing on stages, or next to people or whatever.

TEDDY: I once saw at the Grand Canyon a condor soaring over, and I thought, I must seem so small to him.

ELVIS: I'd like to feel small for a bit. Oh let's go Teddy.

Lights fade.

VIDEO: The following dialogue plays in the video sequence, with TEDDY and ELVIS recreating the finale of THELMA & LOUISE.

As the video plays, ELVIS and TEDDY exit.

NOTE: The rest of the action happens on video.

ELVIS: *(Shouting over the chaos.)* I really like you man!!

TEDDY: Oh, well that's a lovely thing to hear!

ELVIS: I mean it!

TEDDY: Let's be honest! You don't really know me!

ELVIS: Sure I do!

TEDDY: You only know what I have presented to you!

ELVIS: Man! I knew you even before I knew you like I know you now!

Emotional movie theme music begins.

I know your deeds man. And your words. "It is not the critic who counts. The credit belongs to the man who is actually in the arena!"

Emotional music rises.

TEDDY and ELVIS: "There is little use for the being whose tepid soul knows nothing of great and generous emotion, of the high pride, the stern belief, the lofty enthusiasm, of the men who quell the storm and ride the thunder."

VIDEO: TEDDY AND ELVIS DRIVE OFF THE CLIFF. The car soars through the blue sky and music plays until right before the climax when –

Music cuts out, with hard cut to:

VIDEO: ANN at the wall outside of Graceland.

This video is quiet, just the sound of the atmosphere and neighborhood outside Graceland. ANN walks slowly along the wall, surveying the signatures of all those ELVIS has touched.

ANN looks at the house through the gate, which is closed for the day.

Eventually ANN finds a small open spot, on a low corner of the wall. Takes out a marker. Signs "Ann. Thank you."

ANN stands. Closes eyes.

BLACKOUT.

Also by
the TEAM

Five Plays by the TEAM
Give Up! Start Over! (In the darkest of times I look to Richard Nixon for hope) /
A Thousand Natural Shocks / Particularly in the Heartland / Architecting / Mission Drift
9781783191901

Mission Drift
9781783190256

WWW.OBERONBOOKS.COM

 Follow us on www.twitter.com/@oberonbooks
& www.facebook.com/OberonBooksLondon